AF075732

Making the MATCH

Making the MATCH

Tom Watt

Illustrated by
Alan Brown

Collins

Contents

Chapter 1 A team game 2

Player positions 12

Chapter 2 Practice makes perfect 14

Practice, practice, practice! 22

Chapter 3 Football experts 24

The science of sport 32

Chapter 4 Nothing without fans! 34

Football for all! 44

Chapter 5 Matchday 46

Laws of the game..................... 56

Chapter 6 Stars of tomorrow? 58

Glossary 68

About the author 70

About the illustrator................... 72

Book chat 74

Chapter 1
A team game

Football is the world's most popular game. People everywhere play football on pitches, in parks, or even on the street. Millions of fans watch the biggest matches, either in **stadiums** or on TV.

Fact!
There are five billion football fans worldwide. That's more than half the population of the world!

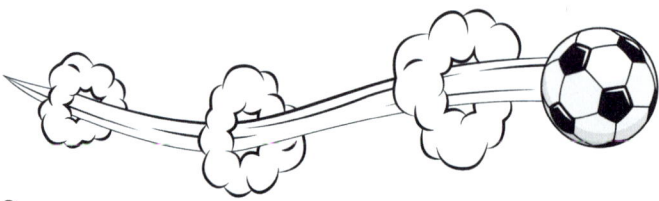

Football matches can be unpredictable, which is part of what makes them exciting! The players' brilliant skills captivate the fans as they cheer their team on. It's an exhilarating experience that people of all ages and backgrounds come together to enjoy. Everyone feels part of the action!

Each team has eleven players on the pitch at any one time. Footballers come in all shapes and sizes. Some players are big and strong, some are tall and skinny and others are short and stocky. Every player has a unique set of skills. They might be really fast runners or brilliant at **passing** the ball to team-mates. They might be good at **tackling**, or being in the right place to score goals. A good team mixes various different skills and qualities together to create a winning formula.

Every team needs an **agile** goalkeeper (the Goalie) who can catch or punch the ball to stop the opposition from scoring. They guard their goal at all costs. Every goalie knows that one mistake might cost their team the game!

In front of the Goalie, the team has a line of defenders. The defenders are experts at stopping the other team from getting near the goal to score. Their job is to defend the goal and try to get the ball off the other team. They love to tackle! If the defenders can get the ball, they'll pass it to their team's midfield players.

The midfielders **dribble** forwards with the ball or kick it towards the attackers. This is when the crowd starts getting excited! The attackers, who are also called strikers, try to score a goal. Can they kick the ball into the net? It's goals that win games, after all!

As well as the eleven players on the pitch, each team also has substitute players. They have to wait at the side of the pitch, ready to join in the game when needed. A substitute might have to replace a team-mate who gets injured or tired. Sometimes substitutes might be called on because the team isn't playing well. Substitutes can bring fresh energy to their team. They might even score the winning goal and be given the 'Player of the Match' award!

One senior player on each team has the extra job of being captain. The captain is the leader of the team, someone the other players respect and listen to. The captain represents their football club, on and off the pitch. They always try to set a good example.

During the game, the captain's job is to talk to their team. They may need to shout to the other players or even tell them off. Usually, though, they try to encourage their team-mates to play at their best.

During a game, the players on the pitch are the centre of the action. They are the people the fans want to see. But have you ever wondered what goes on before a football match can get started? What about all the other jobs that need doing?

There are lots of people who work hard behind the scenes. They are an important part of the football club, too. We're going to meet some of these less well-known heroes in the rest of this book.

Bonus

Player positions

🔴 **Goalkeeper**
The goalie stops the other team scoring.

🔵 **Defenders**
Defenders get the ball for their team.

🟠 **Midfield players**
Midfielders move the ball up the pitch.

🟣 **Attackers**
The strikers shoot for goal!

🟢 Substitutes wait for their chance.

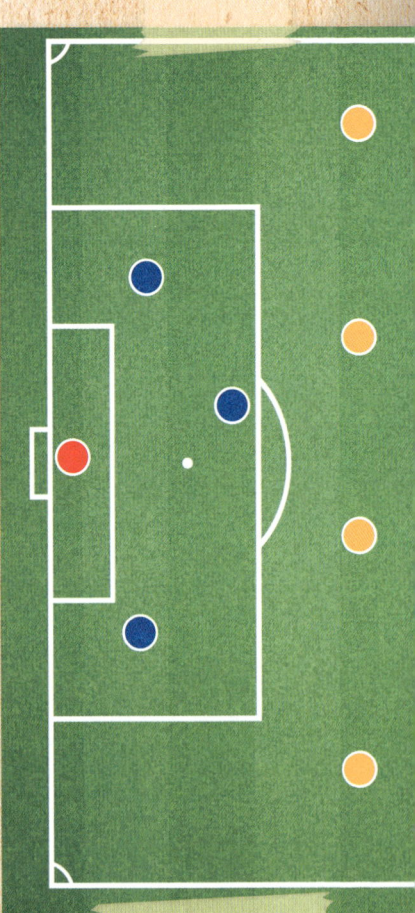

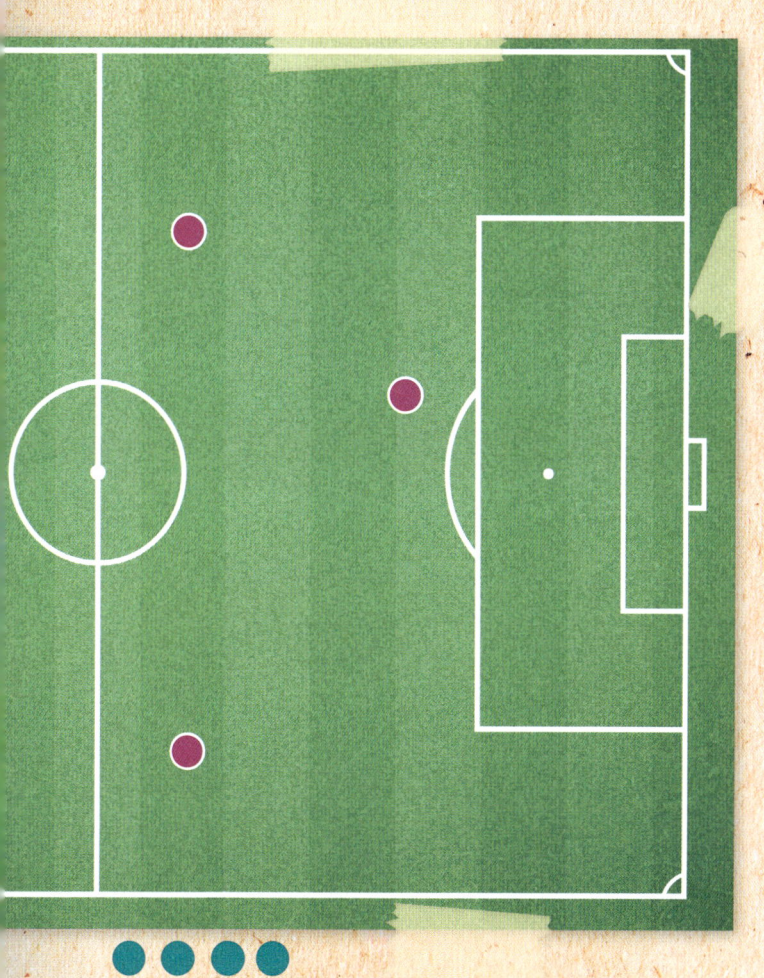

Chapter 2

Practice makes perfect

Footballers play 90-minute matches once or twice each week. That only adds up to around three hours, doesn't it? Have you ever wondered what players do with the rest of their time? Well, every day they're at the training ground practising. They need to keep fit and improve their skills so they're at their absolute best for matches.

There's one person who's in overall charge of the team. They're called the Manager, but the players call them 'Boss'! Managers choose the players and decide how the team will play. If you see someone talking on behalf of a football club on TV, it's usually the Manager.

Each manager has their own way of running a team. Some are strict and a bit scary. Others are calm and persuasive, happy to discuss things with their senior players. Every manager, though, must find a way to inspire the team.

Coaches work with the Manager too. They help the players train. They are like a team behind the team. At a small club, there might only be two or three coaches working with the players. At a top club, though, there might be 20 experts sharing the different jobs around.

First, the Manager and coaches discuss what the players need to work on. The coaches then have to think up training routines. They work out how to put the Manager's plan for winning the next game into action. The coaches vary the routines from day to day. They try to make sure the players practise all their football skills and don't get bored!

Who are the different coaches and what do they do? The First Team Coach plans and leads the training sessions out on the pitch. They make sure that the players work hard.

The players must be fit and strong, too. That's where the Fitness Coach comes in. They are in charge when the players have to do extra running, stretching, and exercising in the gym.

Fact!

A football club's 'first team' is their best group of players.

As well as being fit, the players need to think about upcoming matches. They need to learn to play the way the Manager wants them to play. The coaches make sure the players know what to expect from opposing teams, and have a plan to beat them! Practice makes perfect, right?

Some coaches focus on particular players and positions. For example, the Goalkeeping Coach works with the club's goalkeepers. They spend hours practising saving goals, by punching and catching the ball.

Splosh!

Fact!

Training grounds have football pitches. They have a gym, offices, classrooms and even a cafeteria as well!

The Striker Coach works with the club's attacking players. The coach shows them how to keep the ball when defenders are trying to take it away from them. They teach the strikers the best places to be to score goals. Then the strikers practise until every single shot is on target!

Another important person helping the Manager is the Chief Scout. The Manager is always on the look out for better players. So the Chief Scout goes to watch matches and studies games from **leagues** around the world on TV. They put together a report on every player the Manager might be interested in. If the club is going to pay for a new player, they want to guarantee they'll get value for money!

Before each match, the players and coaches gather in the changing room. The Manager reminds everybody about all the work they've done in training the previous week. Then it's up to the players. It's their job to seize the moment, score some goals, and win the match!

Very skilful and experienced player.
Maybe a little old for our team now!

 **Bonus**

Practice, practice, practice!

Arsenal Women training

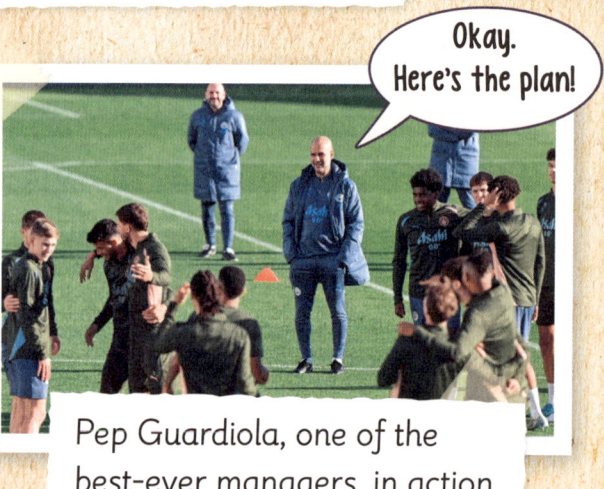

Pep Guardiola, one of the best-ever managers, in action

Goalkeeper training at Hibernian FC

Brighton's players get a team talk.

Chapter 3
Football experts

At the top level, football is a science as well as a game. Teams in the top leagues around the world are very serious about winning. Clubs will do everything they can to be the best.

Experienced managers don't want to rely on guesswork, so how can they make sure their team has the best chances of winning? They need to measure how hard their players are working. They want to gather information from previous matches and find out all they can about the opposition, and that's where science can help.

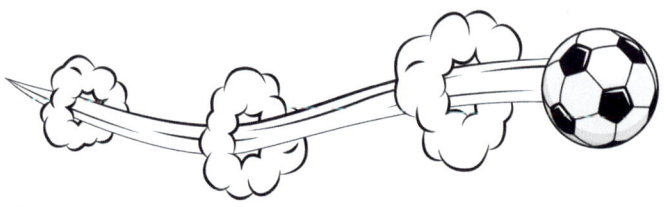

Sports scientists can gather lots of information from training sessions and matches, and decide what it all means. They share this information with the Manager, and can even suggest ways to improve the team's chances of winning. No wonder managers want to work with top experts!

The Sports Scientist has equipment which allows them to track the players' performances. They record each player's speed, heart rate, and their positions on the field. This gives a picture of everything the player does during a game or a training session.

Fact!

Top players wear little computers under their shirts! These devices send messages to the scientists about everything each player does.

Then, the Sports Scientist can tell the Manager how far and how fast each player ran. They can show how high the players jumped and how far they kicked the ball. Did they have lots of **stamina** or did they get tired quickly? The scientist can point out each player's strengths and weaknesses.

Video Analysts study videos of the team's previous games. They see what went well the last time the team played – and what didn't! They will look through hours and hours of videos. Their job is to pick out the important bits for everyone to see. They share video highlights with the players and coaches. Sometimes the analyst can point out bits of skill or little mistakes. These highlights can often give the Manager ideas about how to win the next match. Then the coaches can work with the players during training and make plans to outwit the opposing team.

Top footballers' bodies are like powerful machines, so the fuel they take on is important! Clubs have a Nutritionist to make sure the players are eating the right foods at all times. The Nutritionist carefully plans each player's diet to help them perform at their best. They need protein from meat or fish to give them power. They get carbohydrates from things like rice and pasta for extra stamina. Vegetables and fruit give them vitamins to keep them healthy.

Fact!

Arsenal was the first UK club to put broccoli on the training ground menu every day!

Footballers can sometimes get hurt during matches or in training. So football clubs employ a Physiotherapist (Physio) in case that happens. If a player gets hurt during a game, the Physio runs on to treat them. They have to decide quickly whether an injury is serious or not. Can the Physio help the player and get them back in the game? Or will a substitute need to come on to replace them?

After an injury, the Physio will plan an exercise routine to guide the player's recovery. The routine can combine **massages**, stretching, and strengthening exercises using machines in the gym. Once the Physio decides the player is well enough, they can start running and kicking a ball in training again.

Physios carefully guide a player towards being able to play matches again, using massage and exercise. A good physio will make sure the player doesn't rush, even when the Manager wants to have the team's star player back straight away!

 Bonus

The science of sport

"Over 23 miles per hour? No wonder I can't keep up with you, Micky!"

Micky van de Ven was the Premier League's fastest player in 2024.

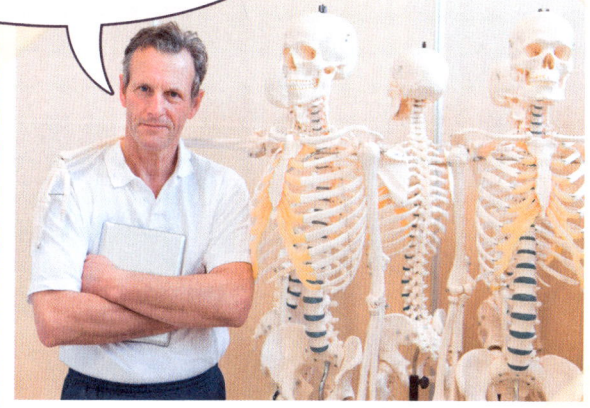

Bad news from the expert!

Physio Vikki Stevens in action

Chapter 4

Nothing without fans!

Big football clubs pay their players to play for them. That's why they need fans to come along and pay money to watch the team in action. Elite clubs have thousands of supporters in the stadium for every match. Lots more people watch the games on TV.

Fact!

Over 80,000 supporters watch every Barcelona FC game at their home stadium in Spain. And guess what? They are now making the stadium even bigger!

Lots of fans like to wear a replica team shirt, or a scarf or hat in their club's colours. That's good for the club, because they can sell those items in their shop or online. The Club Shop Manager is in charge of that.

At smaller clubs, the shop might just be a little wooden hut at the stadium. At top Premier League clubs, the shops are as big as supermarkets! They sell kits, hats, toys, books, watches, even pyjamas and slippers! The Club Shop Manager makes sure everything in the shop has the club's name or badge on it. That's what the fans want!

Fact!

Blue is the most popular colour for football kits, followed by red!

Every football club has its own badge. Most clubs have a Mascot as well, a person who dresses up as an animal or character related to the club. Arsenal's Mascot is a dinosaur called Gunnersaurus, because the club's nickname is 'The Gunners'. Gunnersaurus was invented by two young Arsenal fans who also liked dinosaurs! The Mascot goes around the stadium before games to say hello to the fans and make everyone feel welcome.

Home sweet home for the fans!

Football clubs rely on their fans to support them. In return, most clubs work hard to support their local communities. That's a full-time job for the Head of Community! They organise football sessions for children, for old people, and for people with disabilities. It's important that everyone gets the chance to enjoy playing. The sessions are a chance to make new friends, too.

The Head of Community might also arrange after-school clubs where children can do their homework or play with their friends. Some clubs run courses for young people who have left school and need help to find jobs or get work experience. Sometimes, the Head of Community can persuade the club's players to come along and say hello. That's exciting for everybody!

Getting thousands of fans into the stadium for a big game is a challenge, and so is getting them out again! That's a job for the Stadium Manager. They have to think of everything that could go wrong. Then they make sure that it doesn't! They need to know how many fans will be coming to the game. Is the stadium clean and tidy? Does everyone know what to do in case of a fire? What happens if there's a power cut and all the lights go out?

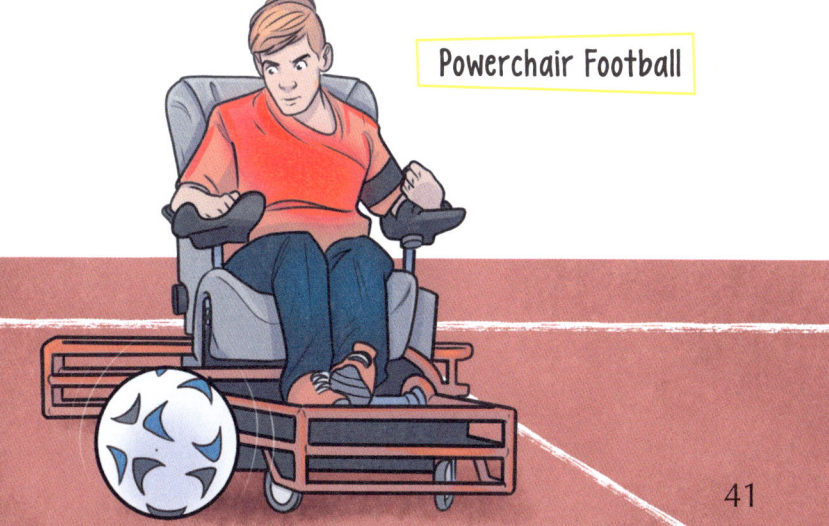

Powerchair Football

On the day of the game, the Stadium Manager has a team of matchday stewards to help. They guide fans to their seats and keep them safe during the match. If fans are in the wrong place or start arguing with each other, the stewards step in. They also make sure nobody runs onto the pitch when a goal is scored!

Fact!

Every single seat in the stadium has its own number! So the number on your ticket tells you where you are going to sit.

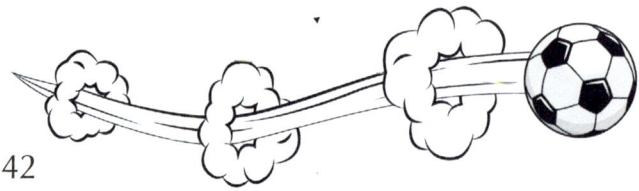

Without the crowd cheering, there would be no atmosphere at games. Without supporters spending money on tickets and **merchandise**, there would be less money to pay the star players. In fact, you could say there would be no football clubs without football fans!

 Bonus

Football for all!

a game at the Powerchair Football World Cup

a Blind Football match at the Paralympics

a Cerebral Palsy Football team training for the Paralympics

West Ham's Down's syndrome team in action against Fulham

Chapter 5
Matchday

Players and fans wake up excited on the day of a game. They are looking forward to kick-off.

Some people, though, are already at the stadium hours before the players and fans get there. They have jobs to do before the game can even start. They may not be famous like the players but, without them, the match can't happen. Let's turn the spotlight on some of them now!

The Groundskeeper is at the stadium every single day. A football pitch is around 100 metres long and about 70 metres wide. That's big! The pitch has to be perfectly flat, and the grass has to be just the right length. A pitch that's in good condition helps players perform at their best!

Groundskeepers have a strict routine. They need to cut the grass and then water it every day.

If there are holes in the pitch, they have to be filled in. If there are bare patches, new grass has to be planted. Luckily, the Groundskeeper has a mower and other machines to help with the work.

A football season lasts nine months, and then the players can have a holiday. But the Groundskeeper can't! Every summer, when matches aren't taking place, they will need to tear up the old pitch and put down a nice new one. They have to guarantee it will be ready for the team to play on when the games begin again.

Fact!

Top clubs have special lights which they can shine on the pitch to help the grass grow. Even at night!

On the day of a game, the Kit Manager is another person who's busy behind the scenes. They have to get all the kit ready for the players, so they're always first to arrive in the changing room.

Each player needs a shirt, shorts, socks, boots and warm-up gear. So do all the substitute players. They all need a spare of everything, too! The Kit Manager brings everything to the stadium on an enormous trolley.

The Kit Manager lays out the clean kit in the empty changing room. They know in advance who's playing and where each player will sit. The kit may vary from game to game because the two teams have to play in different colours. They have to stand out from each other! The Kit Manager has to find out which colour their team is going to need. Thinking ahead is an important part of the job.

home

Fact!

The team playing at home always wears their first-choice kit. The away team has to change, if there's a clash of colours!

away

By the time the teams arrive for a match, there's one other person who will already be there getting ready – the Referee! The Referee and their assistants are called the 'Match Officials'. They are another little team. Without a referee, it's very difficult to have a fair match. They do the job because they love football, even though players and fans don't always love them!

The Referee has to check that their watch is working. Along with everything else, they will have to keep time. Then, before the game, they go round and talk to everyone. They meet the Groundskeeper to check the pitch. They meet the Stadium Manager to make sure everything is safe and ready for the fans to be let into the stadium.

Finally, they speak to the captains of both teams to remind them of the rules!

Out on the pitch, the Referee blows the whistle to start the match. That moment is called 'kick-off'. It's when the fun starts for everybody! Let's hope it's a brilliant game …

 Bonus

Laws of the game

"Remember! I'm in charge here!"

Referees like Rebecca Welch have the job of making sure everyone sticks to the laws of the game.

"Your arm counts as your hand, you know!"

Apart from the goalie, no player is allowed to touch the ball with their hand. If they do, the other team gets a free kick.

It's a foul if a player kicks an opponent instead of the ball, even if it's by mistake.

If a foul is a bad one, the player gets a warning, a yellow card. If it's a dangerous one, the player is shown a red card. That means they are sent off for the rest of the game. Two yellows equal a red card!

Chapter 6
Stars of tomorrow?

Most people who work at football clubs are focused on the next match. They're getting the team, the stadium or the pitch ready. At most clubs, though, there are also people doing jobs that focus on the future. Those people are already planning what the club will be like five or ten years from now!

Fans love watching the stars of today. Declan Rice, Jude Bellingham, Lauren Hemp and Lauren James all have great technique. But how did they become stars? How does a club find the players who will thrill fans in the future? That work happens in the academy – the club's school for young footballers.

Clubs employ Academy Scouts who go out and watch junior and schools matches. The Scouts then invite promising players to train at the club and join the academy. The Academy Coaches will work with those boys and girls a couple of evenings a week, and in school holidays. Of course, the academy players also play in matches, wearing the club colours!

The Academy Coaches prepare young players for senior football. That takes a long time, and a lot of the young players won't go on to play at **elite** level. They might choose to leave football because they get interested in other things. Sometimes the clubs might decide that the young players won't make it in senior football. Even if young players don't get to the top, though, being in an academy is a fantastic experience for them.

Fact!

Academy Scouts can invite children as young as six years old to join the academy!

At 16 years old, the very best players will become Academy Scholars. For the next two to three years, they'll train every day. Instead of football fitting in around school and family life, everything else has to fit in around football! Academy Scholars have to work really hard, but there's still no guarantee of success.

For Academy Scholars, the Education Officer is a very important person. They make sure that the scholars keep studying and taking exams. It's always important for a young player to have something to fall back on if football doesn't work out. The scholars train either in the morning or in the afternoon. They have to go into school for important lessons, though. They also have to do lots of extra homework each evening!

Academy Scholars have to wait till they're 18 years old to find out if the club is going to take them on. It's very rare for a young player to go straight into the first team. Some young players will go off to get experience at a smaller club. They'll play for the smaller club's first team while they are out 'on loan' from the club they started at. The person who arranges those loans is the Loans Manager.

The Loans Manager tries to pick the best team for a young player to join. Then they'll go and watch them play, to check that things are going well. The Loans Manager decides when the young player is ready to come back and join their own club's first team.

Fact!

England star Harry Kane went out on loan to four clubs before he became a first-team footballer!

The academy staff do a crucial job in looking after young players. But another group of people is often even more important — the player's family. Becoming a top footballer is a precarious and unpredictable process. So the help a young player gets from their family is vital.

Everyone needs guidance and love, especially during difficult times. For a young player to be successful, they'll need support from their family, carers and friends, as well as from their football club.

Glossary

agile being able to move and change direction quickly

dribble running with the ball at your feet

elite top level, the best of the best!

leagues competitions to decide who has the best team

massages rubbing tired muscles to make them stop hurting!

merchandise things that are sold in a shop or online

passing kicking the ball to a team-mate

stadiums big buildings with seats where people can watch sport

stamina long-lasting energy

tackling when two players battle each other for the ball

About the author

Have you always been a writer?

No, I used to be an actor. Then I discovered that I enjoyed writing as much as I enjoyed acting. So now I try to do both – but not at the same time!

Tom Watt

What do you like about writing?

I like finding out things I didn't know. Then I enjoy trying to find the right words to explain those things to other people!

Are you a football fan?

I've always loved playing and watching football. I was never a very good player but that didn't stop me trying! Now I'm a bit older, I spend much more time going to see games or watching them on TV with my son.
I grew up in North London, and was always an Arsenal fan. Now I live away from London, I go to watch my local team, Cheltenham Town. They're a small club in a lower league but I still get excited and jump around when we score!

If you could have any job at the football club, what would you love to do?

Well, I know I was never good enough to be a player! For nearly 40 years, though, I volunteered with Arsenal's community department. So, if I could choose, I'd do that as a job. Football can really make life better for people and I'd like to help to do that.

Why did you want to write this book?

I know lots of people who work in football. Not just players and managers but also those people behind the scenes who do their best but never get much credit. I wanted to celebrate them. I hope it's interesting to read about what they do and why they do it.

What do you hope readers will get from the book?

Everybody knows about famous players and managers. I hope that this book shines a light on all the other people who make football matches possible. Those people all play their part and love the game. It would be great if reading about them made you love football even more, too!

About the illustrator

Have you always been an illustrator?

I've always been an illustrator at heart, but perfecting styles and techniques takes time. Research, practice and pushing boundaries are the key to becoming good.

Alan Brown

How did you get into illustrating?

Since reading comic books in my Gran's sweet shop, I've been hooked on graphics, illustration, characters and stories. It was always my ambition to join this world where imagination and hard work is valued. I gave it my all to get there. Starting in London, working with some renowned illustrators, I learned from some of the greats. I worked my way back up to the North East, to my roots, as a freelance illustrator. I settled in my studio with my favourite comics, toys and studio dog, Otto.

What do you like most about illustrating?

Every brief and script is unique, and I'm trusted with bringing another person's imagination to life. It's the collaboration of writer and illustrator working together that's the most interesting.

Do you use photographs to illustrate from, or your imagination?

It depends on the client's request. They often have a strong sense of how they want characters to look. Sometimes characters are based on photos, and sometimes they have a more cartoony look. In most cases I use a little bit of both – photos for reference, and also imagination.

Do you prefer illustrating fiction or non-fiction books?

I don't think it matters if the book is fiction or non fiction. It's the quality of the narrative that matters. Magic lives in both worlds.

Are you a football fan? Who do you support?

Growing up in the North East, I was born between two strong clubs. You can't help but be pulled into the excitement and passion we have for our teams.

Book chat

Have you read a book like this before?

Have you ever seen a football match?

What was the most interesting thing you learned while reading this book?

What job from this book would you most like to try? Why?

If you had to think of a new title for this book, what would you choose and why?

If you could ask the author anything, what would you ask?

How would you sum up this book in one sentence?

Who would you recommend this book to and why?

Book challenge:
Write a job advert for any job at the football club.

Published by Collins
An imprint of HarperCollins*Publishers*

The News Building
1 London Bridge Street
London
SE1 9GF
UK

Macken House
39/40 Mayor Street Upper
Dublin 1
D01 C9W8
Ireland

© HarperCollins*Publishers* Limited 2025

10 9 8 7 6 5 4 3 2 1

ISBN 978-0-00-874635-3

All rights reserved. No part of this publication may be reproduced, stored in a retrieval system, or transmitted in any form or by any means, electronic, mechanical, photocopying, recording or otherwise, without the prior written permission of the Publisher or a licence permitting restricted copying in the United Kingdom issued by the Copyright Licensing Agency Ltd, 5th Floor, Shackleton House, 4 Battle Bridge Lane, London SE1 2HX.

Without limiting the author's and publisher's exclusive rights, any unauthorised use of this publication to train generative artificial intelligence (AI) technologies is expressly prohibited. HarperCollins also exercise their rights under Article 4(3) of the Digital Single Market Directive 2019/790 and expressly reserve this publication from the text and data mining exception.

British Library Cataloguing-in-Publication Data
A catalogue record for this publication is available from the British Library.

Download the teaching notes and
word cards to accompany this book at:
http://littlewandle.org.uk/signupfluency/

Get the latest Collins Big Cat news at
collins.co.uk/collinsbigcat

Author: Tom Watt
Illustrator: Alan Brown (Advocate Art)
Publisher: Laura White
Product managers: Caroline Green and
　　Holly Woolnough
Series editor: Charlotte Raby
Phonics consultant: Catherine Baker
Commissioning editor and
　　project manager: Emily Hooton
Copyeditor: Sally Byford
Proofreader: Catherine Dakin
Cover designer: Sarah Finan
Typesetter: 2Hoots Publishing Services Ltd
Production controller: Katharine Willard

Printed in the UK.

MIX
Paper | Supporting
responsible forestry
FSC™ C007454

This book contains FSC™ certified paper and other controlled sources to ensure responsible forest management.

For more information visit: www.harpercollins.co.uk/green

Made with responsibly sourced
paper and vegetable ink

Scan to see how we are reducing
our environmental impact.

Acknowledgements
The publishers gratefully acknowledge the permission granted to reproduce the copyright material in this book. Every effort has been made to trace copyright holders and to obtain their permission for the use of copyright material. The publishers will gladly receive any information enabling them to rectify any error or omission at the first opportunity.

p2t grey_and/Shutterstock, p2b Virtis/Shutterstock, pp12–13 prapann/Shutterstock, p13 Angela Ksen/Shutterstock, p22t PA Images/Alamy, p22b News Images LTD/Alamy, p23t 2E9KJ8Y/Alamy, p23b James Boardman/Alamy, p32 IOIO IMAGES/Shutterstock, p33t Juice Flair/Shutterstock, p33b Simon Dack/Alamy, p44t WENN Rights Ltd/Alamy, p44b Victor Velter/Shutterstock, p45t christopher jones/Alamy, p45b PA Images/Alamy, p56t MI News & Sport/Alamy, p56b PA Images/Alamy, p57t PA Images/Alamy, p57b PA Images/Alamy.